Unlocking the Power of Social Media in Healthcare

Table of Contents

The art of medicine consists of amusing the patient while nature cures the disease.

Chapter 1. Introduction

Unveiling the kaleidoscopic expanses of social media today has become as crucial as reading an EKG in the contemporary healthcare landscape. Welcome to our latest Special Report, "Unlocking the Power of Social Media in Healthcare." This comprehensive guide embarks on a riveting exploration of how social platforms are revolutionizing the realms of healthcare, serving as conductors linking medical professionals, patients, and health-impacting information dynamically. Sure, social media is far from a stethoscope, but in this digital era, it's forging pathways toward a more communicative, responsive, and patient-centric medical sphere. If the future of healthcare tickles your curiosity or the harmony of technology and medicine is your symphony, don't miss out on this journey exploring the symbiotic relationship of Social Media and Healthcare. Empower yourself with the knowledge in this special report, as it offers a cheerful yet incisive peep into how these passionate pixels are subtly shaping our well-being narratives. Your dose of enlightenment is just a click away! Don't wait, grab your copy of this special report today!

Chapter 2. The Nexus of Social Media and Healthcare: A Brief Introduction

In the ever-evolving blend of technology and everyday life, an unlikely but powerful connection has come into being, one that demonstrates the permeating capabilities of digitized platforms and their transformative potential: the nexus of social media and healthcare. At first blush, you may find yourself pondering the compatibility of these two disparate entities. But, as you'll soon discover, this convergence is more than a mere collision of worlds; it's opening new vistas in care delivery, patient engagement, and health communication.

2.1. A Brave New World: The Emergence of Social Media

The advent of social media can be traced back to the early 21st century, with platforms like Facebook and Twitter marking their digital footprints and heralding the dawn of an era of unprecedented connectivity. These platforms quickly grew in popularity, creating a global network that fostered a new medium for communication, discourse, and information sharing.

From casual conversations to significant political movements, their impact was far-reaching. However, it wasn't long before the ripples of this digital revolution permeated the hallowed halls of healthcare, unearthing a fascinating confluence of the social and the medical.

2.2. Machinations of Social Media in Healthcare

On the surface, the application of social media within the medical community may seem somewhat superfluous or potentially frivolous. After all, the realm of healthcare, characterized by its stringent protocols and scientific rigor, seemingly stands in stark contrast to the casual, colorful landscape of the digital social world.

However, dig a bit deeper, and you find the genius behind this intersection. It's not about co-opting the latest digital trends for the sake of modernity. Rather, it's leveraging their inherent strengths: accessibility, connectivity, and informational flow.

+ Patient engagement has undergone a 'digital transformation,' creating platforms for two-way interaction between health consumers and providers, enriching the patient-practitioner relationship. + Health literacy, never before so easy to access or distribute, offers opportunities to promote public health campaigns, diffuse crucial health updates, and educate the broader populace on key health indicators. + Platforms for professional collaboration let healthcare providers exchange ideas, share clinical experience, and collectively address pressing healthcare challenges.

These aren't mere conjectures but tangible benefits, each forming an integral strand of the intricate social media-healthcare fabric.

2.3. Perils and Promises: Navigating this New Terrain

Of course, while the possibilities are exciting, this is not a realm devoid of risk, often the gray area like privacy implications, ethical consequences, and validity concerns of health information abound. How do we ensure the accuracy of disseminated health information?

How will patient confidentiality be preserved amidst the 'share culture'? These are areas of critical issues that demand thoughtful deliberation and sound frameworks.

Simultaneously, the potential in harnessing this interface is unrivaled. If navigated adeptly, we could reshape medical practice, redefine patient-provider ties, and reinvent health education. It's a nexus teeming with challenges and opportunities, and it warrants our attention.

2.4. Nearing the Horizon

As a curtain-raiser to the enigmatic tapestry of social media and healthcare, this delve offers a glimpse into this novel yet rapidly maturing realm. Looming ahead is an in-depth exploration of its various facets, from its potential to empower patients to the legalities that surround it.

Dive deep into this confluence of the social media world with medical science, a place where pixels meet the heartbeats, where hashtags intermingle with health indices, and where posts and tweets carry the potential to redefine conventional healthcare paradigms. Indeed, we stand at the forefront of an exciting era; the path meanders, the landscape morphs, and the journey to discover the power of social media in healthcare has just begun. Dive in, for there is much to learn, and, more importantly, much that this nexus can teach us about making healthcare more accessible, more engaging, and more patient-centered.

Heightened engagement, enriched health literacy, collaborative professional growth, all coupled with the challenges of unwrapping the risks – this is the unfolding panorama of the social media and healthcare nexus. What the chapters ahead hold in store beckons you to keep reading and uncovering the promises and pitfalls of this brave new world. Stay tuned, for the exploration is as much about understanding this new facet of healthcare as it is about leveraging it to shape a promising health landscape in the digital age.

Chapter 3. Patient Empowerment: People's Voice in the Digital Age

Unleashing a groundbreaking sea of change, the advent of social media has provided a potent avenue for people's voices, particularly patient voices, to be amplified and heard. It's a digital platform that has emboldened ordinary individuals, especially those struggling with health anomalies, to assume greater control over their health journeys. It is intriguing how these online avenues, which started as a means of connecting people, have now evolved into a powerful tool of empowerment in the healthcare realm.

3.1. The Digital Pandora's Box: Extent of Patient Empowerment

Peering into the vast possibilities that social media can wield in empowering patients, one quickly comes across a multi-faceted landscape. From swaying healthcare decisions, seeking expert opinions, to sharing and comparing health experiences, social media caters to myriad elements of patient empowerment. A study conducted by The Pew Internet & American Life Project in 2019 found that over 80% of Internet users have looked online for health-related information, highlighting the broad influence of the medium.

3.2. Social Media: Peer-to-Peer Healthcare

A significant dimension of patient empowerment brought about by social media is peer-to-peer healthcare. Patients and caregivers are leveraging digital resources to connect with others experiencing similar health concerns. Encouraging the growth of informal, yet impactful communities of patients, these platforms facilitate exchange of health experiences and advice, fostering a supportive network that supplements traditional healthcare mechanisms.

3.3. The Many Faces of Social Media in Health Empowerment

Fitting squarely into the empowerment narrative, various social media platforms serve specific needs. Facebook groups provide a venue for patients and their loved ones to engage in collective discussions, share personal anecdotes and even organize events. On the other hand, Twitter breathes life into health advocacy with hashtags promoting disease awareness or lobbying for health policies. Platforms like Reddit and HealthUnlocked host a plethora of health-related forums, offering users a space to converse anonymously about their experiences and concerns, lending a therapeutic value to digital conversations.

3.4. Real-time Patient Support: Social Media's Crowning Glory

One cannot overlook the role of social media in delivering real-time patient support. In the face of a critical diagnosis or a prevailing health emergency, social media channels emerge as a timely lifeline, connecting patients with the healthcare system and fellow patients in real-time. This immediate exchange of information, advice, and support is a salient feature of social media, bolstering patient confidence and autonomy at a substantial level.

3.5. Driving Health Literacy: Wise Patients in the Digital Age

The empowerment wave reverberating through social media also fuels health literacy. Relevant health information disseminated through social media channels aids in dispelling medical myths and promoting accurate health knowledge. However, the concern for the authenticity of information courses through the veins of the digital healthcare world and requires stringent checks to prevent misinformation.

3.6. Implications and Cautions: Navigating the Digital Landscape

While social media has undoubtedly sparked a new era for patient empowerment, it is still a realm brimming with intricacies and ambiguities. Information privacy, unreliable content, and negative emotional impact are among the challenging aspects to be navigated. As we rejoice in the empowerment rendered by social media, it's paramount to foster digital health literacy and adhere to ethical guidelines to reduce potential risks.

3.7. Future Projections: Thriving in the Digital Proliferation

As we thread the needle of the future, the synergy of social media and healthcare is expected to evolve further. Further research and discussions on ethical practises, data privacy, and standards for the assessment of digital health applications can foster safer and more beneficial platforms for patient empowerment.

Stepping into the digital age has redefined the interactions between patients, healthcare professionals, and health systems. No longer are patients passive recipients of care; they are active participants moulding their healthcare experiences. In the grand dance of healthcare evolution, social media is not merely a spectating audience, but an essential choreographer directing the rhythm and movements of patient empowerment. With its ability to amplify voices and transform patient experiences, social media indeed has reframed healthcare engagement in the digital age.

Chapter 4. Healthcare Professionals on Social Platforms: Pros, Cons and Potential

The potential of leveraging social media as a key tool in the wide spectrum of healthcare continues to gain traction in our increasingly interconnected digital age. The marriage of social media outlets and healthcare invites a myriad of exciting prospects; nevertheless, these opportunities arguably dwell arm in arm with compelling challenges that can't be ignored or lightly dismissed.

4.1. The Prospects of Healthcare Professionals on Social Platforms

First and foremost, let's delve into the advantages of this relationship between healthcare professionals and social media platforms. Social media channels offer a platform for networking and communication among healthcare providers. It allows a seamless exchange of scientific knowledge, medical trends, relevant research findings, and healthcare-related dialogues amongst colleagues and like-minded professionals. This unfettered access to an ocean of knowledge-sharing pushes the boundaries of traditional medical education and training modalities while fostering higher levels of competencies and skill enrichment.

Moreover, social media provides an interactive platform from where healthcare professionals can disseminate health-related information to a vast audience effectively and swiftly. Public health announcements, awareness campaigns, medical breakthrough information, crisis management updates, and other vital health narratives can reach an unprecedented number of people by capitalizing on the inherent virality mechanisms that many of these platforms offer. From a public health perspective, the potential of social media to connect professionals with the populace at large is astounding.

One cannot ignore the immense potential social media brings in forming a patient-centered approach. Enabling patients to voice their health experiences, seek peer support, and better understand their health conditions more transparently can lead to a more empowered patient populace. Social media, used correctly, may lead healthcare professionals to derive a holistic understanding of their patients' perspectives and pain points. These insights, when incorporated into care delivery models, can essentially enhance patient satisfaction, engagement, and overall health outcomes.

4.2. The Professional Challenges and Potential Downfalls on Social Platforms

Despite the glittering attraction the aforementioned advantages present, healthcare professionals need to thread cautiously in the often complicated and forever evolving landscape of social media. The blurring of professional boundaries is a key concern. Personal and professional boundaries may dissolve when healthcare practitioners interact with patients or share personal life snippets on these platforms. This could potentially lead to ethical dilemmas, breach of trust, confidentiality issues, and unforeseen disagreements.

Privacy and confidentiality violations are another grey area where even the most cautious healthcare providers might inadvertently stumble upon using social platforms. Private patient information that finds its way onto these platforms, either intentionally or accidentally, can invite serious implications concerning noncompliance with regulatory standards like HIPAA (Health Insurance Portability and Accountability Act). Protecting patients' privacy and safeguarding their sensitive health information is both a legal obligation and a professional expectation each healthcare provider must steadfastly adhere to, regardless of the digital platform's conveniences.

The potential for misinformation also looms large. For as beautiful as the digital realm can be, it can also be a hotbed for misinformation, half-truths, and outlandish health claims. Healthcare professionals must tread this delicate balance of promoting accurate health information while actively combating medical misinformation that can have potentially harmful or even dangerous consequences.

4.3. The Potentialities and Future Exploration

Despite these challenges, the potential for the use of social media in healthcare settings demonstrates a promising future brimming with opportunities for exploration. However, effective implementation, it could be argued, requires stringent professional and ethical guidelines promoting the responsible use of social media platforms by healthcare professionals. A well-designed social media policy with clearly outlined standards of conduct, patient privacy safeguards, and a clear redressal mechanism for breaching these standards can serve as a robust beginning point.

Moreover, harnessing the power of AI-driven data analytics tools can help healthcare professionals strategically use social media platforms for research and insights. This way, the potential for learning about patient behaviors, tracking disease trends, and understanding public health threats can be fully harnessed, providing a rich source of information that could fortify patient-care strategies.

At the end of the day, like any powerful tool, social media comes with its share of challenges and opportunities. A skilled craftsman, well aware of the tool's potency, can wield it effectively and responsibly only by understanding the risks, limitations, and potential benefits associated with it.

In conclusion, the integration of healthcare professionals onto social media platforms paints a captivating picture of the future, one that oscillates between immense promise and considerable challenge. Yet, the power of this dynamic relationship between healthcare and social media is indisputable. As we continue to explore these synergies, we must tread carefully to capitalize on the benefits while safeguarding against risks, ensuring the integrity of personalized patient care remains at the heart of the digital health revolution.

Chapter 5. Case Studies: Transformative Healthcare Upgrades by Social Media

The transformative potential of social media in healthcare has often been discussed in the abstract or theoretical sense; through optimistic forecasts and technological conjectures. To cement these ideas into the tangible reality, the exploration of numerous case studies where social media demonstrated clear, measurable, positive impacts in the healthcare arena becomes indispensable.

5.1. The Mayo Clinic: Championing Patient Engagement Through Social Media

One of the early adopters of social media in healthcare, Mayo Clinic started employing these platforms back in 2008 to augment its communications with patients. Since then, they've created a myriad of communities online where their patients share their stories and experiences, find support, and learn from each other.

An example that illuminates the immense value of these networks can be found in the decision by Mayo Clinic to conduct a social media campaign to facilitate transplant discussions. The campaign encouraged patients to share their organ donation stories through the hashtag #TransplantHope, a seemingly simple activity that grew to have profound impacts on organ donation awareness and registrations.

The clinic also developed the Mayo Clinic Social Media Network (MCSMN) to empower other healthcare organizations, providing resources, training and tools to build their own social media health communities online. This proactive step underlines the commitment of Mayo clinic to leverage social media to extend improvements in patient care beyond their immediate network.

5.2. King's College Hospital (KCH), London: Driving Patient Rehabilitation Through YouTube

King's College Hospital took to YouTube to bridge the post-treatment guidance gap, creating a series of videos demonstrating physiotherapy workouts that patients can follow at home after their treatment. This initiative was especially beneficial for patients unable to attend regular follow-ups due to distance or physical limitations.

An evaluation of this intervention revealed a significant positive impact on patient adherence to physiotherapy regimes, alleviating rehabilitation headaches for the hospital and encouraging faster recovery for patients. This innovative use of a popular social media platform reflects the versatility of such networks in performing tasks more effectively, which were previously deemed challenging by traditional methods.

5.3. Cincinnati Children's Hospital: Using Facebook Live for Information Dissemination

Cincinnati Children's Hospital transformed their Facebook page into an active hub of information by utilizing the Facebook Live feature to host interactive sessions. Parents and caregivers were able to tune in to these live video broadcasts that included discussions on crucial childcare topics and live Q&A sessions with health care professionals.

Engagement on these sessions was impressive, drawing an average viewer count of about 2,500. As a result, the hospital was able to offer necessary information accessibly, achieving a widespread reach that would have been difficult through the traditional communication channels.

Through these examples, it becomes evident not only that social media provides an array of unique opportunities, but also that success lies as much in creativity and innovation, as in understanding the underlying networks and their possibilities. Each case study demonstrates social media's capacity to involve patients more directly in their healthcare journey, shedding light on areas for future exploration and development.

Such transformative examples show us that the impacts of social media in healthcare are not theoretical predictions or optimistic dreams; they are unfolding in real-time, providing incredible upgrades to patient care, education, and empowerment. A future in which persons are connected with their healthcare processes in personalized and impactful ways seems not just possible, but inevitable. And, the most exciting part? This is only the beginning. We have barely scratched the surface on the ways that healthcare can leverage social media to its benefit. The digital healthcare revolution is here to stay!

Chapter 6. Data Privacy and Confidentiality: The Gray Areas of Social Health Networks

As we set sail on the vast sea of data privacy and confidentiality within the realm of social health networks, it is important to first understand that these sophisticated digital tools serve a dichotomous master. One side is the marvel of seamless communication, postulated by the concept of a shared electronic health records system or social health network, empowering patients and healthcare providers alike with enhanced access and control while promoting competent collaboration in the healthcare spectrum. The other side, often the underbelly of this communication wonder, reveals a cornucopia of concerns related to data privacy, security, and confidentiality. Striking the right balance is our predicament and mission.

6.1. The Imperative for Data Privacy

Data privacy, essentially being the right to have one's data utilized in specific, consented ways by specified entities, is an emergent concern in the increasingly digital-centric facet of healthcare. This entails keeping personal health data secure from unauthorized access, modification, or dissemination. A significant chunk of population engaging with healthcare providers via social media or related digital platforms unknowingly leave behind a digital footprint that can affect their privacy. As the custodians of such data, the onus falls on healthcare providers and the platforms themselves to ensure these digital trails are appropriately safeguarded.

Getting down to the crux of the matter, data privacy and security concerns arise due to a number of reasons. These include increased data sharing and storage, more parties getting access to data, the commercial value of health data, threats from cyber-attacks and data breaches, and potential misuses of sensitive patient data. Inadvertent leakage or theft of this data can lead to severe implications such as identity theft, financial fraud, or even subjection to various forms of discrimination.

6.2. The Ethical Challenges

At this juncture, it's worth delving deeper into the ethical challenges that emerge as a by-product of the confluence between healthcare and social media. Healthcare professionals, while mining the power of these platforms, also must grapple with maintaining patient confidentiality, adhering to professional boundaries, and dealing with the life-long permanence of digital dialogue. Consent is another ethical challenge recently coming into the limelight, especially when dealing with vulnerable populations or those unable to provide informed consent such as children or individuals with certain cognitive impairments. On the other hand, equivocal regulations concerning disclosure policies and data ownership only add fuel to the skepticism fire.

6.3. Legal Nuances and Challenges

The legal landscape pertaining to data privacy, sharing, and ownership in the virtual healthcare domain has yet to mature. While regulations like the Health Insurance Portability and Accountability Act (HIPAA) in the US or the General Data Protection Regulation (GDPR) in the European Union are making strides in promoting data privacy and patients' rights, enforcement remains variable and often weak. The dynamic and evolving nature of these platforms further complicates the issue. Adjusting to digital advances and ensuring patient's rights necessitate constant revision and interpretation of laws, which takes time.

6.4. The Role of Health Information Technology

Health Information Technology (HIT) serves as both a boon and bane in the data privacy debate. On the bright side, advances in HIT have mitigated several data privacy concerns. Blockchain technology, for instance, offers a promising solution to data security issues, and also can upend the traditional centralized data exchange, ensuring improved data privacy. Encryption technology, two-factor authentication, biometric data scanners, data anonymizing services, and advanced firewalls are similar measures that deserve a mention.

Yet, the optimization of these measures remains problematic, and ongoing concerns persist around data breaches due to human error or sophisticated cyber-attacks, key threats that HIT must continue to address.

6.5. Future Steps: A Call for Vigilance

The healthcare landscape, in accordance with its digital metamorphosis, is urged to fortify its data privacy and confidentiality mechanisms through a synergy of technology, law, and ethics. Regular audits, robust data security systems, timely updates, and employee training could be potential starting points. A culture entrenched in data privacy norms and regulations, coupled with severe penalties for breaches, will go a long way in fostering trust amongst users.

In a nutshell, social health networks gatekeeping vast troves of personal data must uphold the apothegm of "With great power comes great responsibility." Willing or not, they are stepping into the role of guardians of sensitive, potentially life-altering information and should be held to the highest standards. In this delicate dance between connectivity and confidentiality, every step taken must be deliberate and nuanced, keeping patient well-being and privacy at the forefront. As daunting a task as it may seem, the requirement for this balance is nothing short of imperative in maintaining the integrity of healthcare delivery in the digital age. Today, in the grey areas of social health networks, we are standing at a threshold, witnessing a paradigm shift in patient empowerment, healthcare delivery, and data privacy norms. The onus is on us, as stakeholders, to ensure that this shift remains beneficial for all involved, never losing sight of the human element at our core.

As we embark on the digital future of healthcare, the above implications serve as a sobering reminder of our responsibilities. To stay afloat in this vast sea of information, we must keep our compass firmly directed towards a future that upholds the sanctity of data privacy and confidentiality, while harnessing the power of social health networks to their fullest potential.

Chapter 7. Digital Health Marketing: Social Media as the New Frontier

In recent years, the digital landscape has effectuated a remarkable shift from traditional marketing techniques to tech-driven strategies for enchanting audiences and expanding brand reach. This change has been particularly momentous for healthcare industries as they attempt to leverage the power of social media. This chapter will delve deep into an engaging discourse about the advent of Digital Health Marketing, how it has become a transformative frontier for the healthcare ecosystem, and the considerable potential it holds.

7.1. Unleashing the New Terrain: Social Media as a Marketing Force

Social media, with its vast network of interconnected users providing instantaneous communication and engagement, has emerged as a powerful force in the marketing sector, propelling healthcare brands to consider it a principal avenue for outreach.

In essence, digital health marketing allows healthcare providers to use digital tools and technologies to advertise and promote their services, engage with the public, and create a stronger rapport with their clientele. This is achieved via various popular social media platforms, such as Facebook, Twitter, Instagram, LinkedIn, and more. These digital venues proffer a multitude of benefits, such as an expanded audience base, a dynamic two-way communication channel, and data-driven capabilities for an immersive, personalized user experience.

One crucial aspect that differentiates digital health marketing from traditional means is the data-backed, tailored approach. The ability to utilize analytics for targeting specific demographics and analyzing consumer behavior offers a more customized, relevant, and successful marketing crusade.

7.2. Transforming Patient Engagement: Interaction and Authenticity

Potent utilization of social media in health marketing has led to a quantum leap in patient engagement. The interactive nature of these platforms encourages active participation from the viewers, moving away from one-way communication to an interactive dialogue. For instance, healthcare providers can post informative blogs about prevalent health issues or offer live interactions to address user queries, which results in spreading awareness, boosting patient confidence, and fostering a sense of community.

7.3. Tracking Success Metrics: Data-Driven Decisions

The pivotal attribute that cybernetic platforms offer to digital health marketers is the ability to assess campaign effectiveness through various indicators like engagement rate, impressions, conversions, etc. This quantitative edge provides an insight into what resonates with the audience and what needs improvement, making marketing strategies smarter and more target-specific. Further, advanced algorithms and machine learning can enable predictive marketing, giving health marketers a crystal ball-like insight into future trends.

7.4. The Efficacy of Influencer Marketing in Healthcare

An offshoot of digital health marketing that is gaining traction is influencer marketing. Tapping into the popularity of social media influencers to endorse healthcare products or services has an organic appeal that feels less intrusive. It also allows brands to reach specific demographics and engage with audiences that they might not have tapped into otherwise.

7.5. Vulnerabilities and Challenges

While the benefits of digital health marketing are colossal, it is imperative to acknowledge its associated challenges. The same communication transparency that favourably supports an open dialogue can turn counterproductive if negative feedback or misinformation is circulated. Therefore, adroit navigation and diligent crisis management on social media platforms are paramount.

Moreover, compliance with regulatory norms and laws like HIPAA (Health Insurance Portability and Accountability Act) in the US, or GDPR (General Data Protection Regulation) in the EU, is a critical concern, given the sensitive nature of health information.

7.6. The Road Ahead

The convergence of social media in healthcare marketing has undoubtedly set a new benchmark. However, the road ahead requires continuous fine-tuning and evolution. This includes the discerning adoption of emerging technologies like AI, virtual reality, augmented reality in marketing strategies, and more importantly, maintaining trust and transparency throughout this digital journey.

From creating awareness to driving patient engagement, digital health marketing on social media has created a paradigm shift in the healthcare sphere. While the dynamic nature of this field presents challenges that demand agility and adaptability, the opportunities it unfolds are simply transformative for healthcare providers. With sound strategies and ethical lineaments, this digital frontier hints at a promising future, and rightfully so, in enhancing healthcare accessibility and effectiveness for one and all.

Chapter 8. Regulations and Legalities: Navigating the Cyber Healthcare Terrain

As we delve into the vast landscapes of social media utilization in healthcare, the essential role of regulations and legalities stands out, serving as the cardinal pillars of an engaged, safe and meaningful online medical environment. Safeguarding professional standards, patient privacy, and ensuring reliable information dissemination, these constraints become crucial keys to responsibly navigate the uncharted terrains of cyber healthcare.

8.1. The Landscape of Legalities and Regulations

If we liken social media in healthcare to a sprawling, vibrant cityscape, then the regulations and legalities form its intricate city blueprint—abstract lines and symbols that instruct us how we should construct and inhabit this bustling cyber metropolis responsibly. From General Data Protection Regulation (GDPR) to the Health Insurance Portability and Accountability Act (HIPAA) in the U.S. to stricter data localization laws in countries like Russia and China, the international regulatory landscape is interspersed with nation-specific requirements and global privacy norms. Understanding the specifics of these regulations is imperative in creating an inviting yet secure digital healthcare environment.

8.2. Utilizing HIPAA in a Digital World

The HIPAA has become the ethical and legal cornerstone guiding the handling of health information in the United States. Under this legislation, healthcare practitioners and establishments must adhere to stringent regulations about the use, disclosure, and safeguarding of patient data. Social media, due to its very nature, presents unique challenges in maintaining these standards. For instance, sharing case details over a Facebook Live session or tweeting patient updates run the risk of violating HIPAA conditions. To avow compliance, meticulous care must be exercised in training healthcare staff about HIPAA mandates, underlining the significance of confidentiality, obtaining informed consent from patients, and using secure channels for communication.

8.3. GDPR: A Pan-European Solution

Across the pond, the European Union has its General Data Protection Regulation (GDPR) that centers around bolstering data rights of its denizens, mandating explicit consent, data minimization, right to erasure, and data portability among other considerations. GDPR invariably stirs social media use in healthcare, necessitating that organizations craft holistic strategies to comply with its detailed stipulations. This may involve implementing secure data storage solutions, stress-testing existing policies, or enhancing patient awareness about their data rights.

8.4. Nation-Specific Constraints

Often, national laws inject specific requirements for data handling, way beyond the provisions of international norms. For instance, in Russia and China, data localization laws require that citizen data be stored within the country, demanding extensive infrastructural adaptation. Then there are countries with strict cyber defamation provisions, making it incumbent upon healthcare providers to ensure the information shared across their social channels is factual, accurate, and devoid of defamatory or slanderous content.

8.5. Tackling Infodemics: The Regulatory Quandary

Regulations aren't solely about personal data protection. They also play an active role in combating 'infodemics' — an overabundance of accurate and inaccurate information that makes it harder for people to find trustworthy sources and guidance when needed. To address this, platforms like Facebook, Instagram, and Twitter, often sweep their platforms to quell misinformation. However, discerning the difference between unverified, possibly harmful content, and censorship has proven to be a tricky regulatory tightrope.

8.6. Navigating the Regulatory Terrain: Concluding Thoughts

To conclude, regulations and legality form the lynchpin ensuring symbiotic cohabitation within the sprawling cityscape of social media in healthcare. They ensure that while we drive innovation and connectivity, we do not lose sight of individual liberties, data rights, and the truth. Correctly understanding and implementing these guidelines is tantamount to establishing a safe, effective, and ethical digital healthcare system. As we continue to evolve in our use of social media within healthcare, so too must our understanding and application of these regulatory frameworks to maintain a delicate balance between service, security, and innovation.

Chapter 9. Future Projections: The Road Ahead for Social Media in Healthcare

Our journey into the exploration of the future of social media's imprints on healthcare commences in a technicolor ferment, featuring a contemplative yet confident gaze onto forthcoming perspectives. As cyber waves gradually replace corridors, we witness an intriguing metamorphosis in patient-centric care settings.

9.1. Advancements and Evolution on the Horizon

Looking ahead to the near future, a plethora of advancements in technology and healthcare, integrated through social media, are prudently eyeing diverse scenarios. More sophisticated Artificial Intelligence (AI) algorithms would tango with social media interfaces, creating a smarter, more precise, predictive, and proactive healthcare environment. On top of that, more widespread utilization of telemedicine and virtual reality are compelling certainties.

Envision a world where AI integrated with social media not only aids in understanding patient needs but predicts them. Patients might report symptoms, receive diagnostic suggestions, and book appointments, all greeted by an AI on their trusted social media platform. Furthermore, the dawn of wearable tech integrated with social media is on the horizon, with advancements envisioned to monitor, collect, and transmit of real-time health data, enabling swift medical feedback for patients.

9.2. Future Models of Patient Care

Our glance at the future also incorporates shifts in patient care models. Take a leap and imagine patients with chronic diseases effectively managing the symptoms with the help of peer support groups on social media. Each patient can share their unique experiences and coping strategies, offering invaluable insights to others combating similar fights — picturing the realm of patient empowerment in its splendid form.

Other future perspectives include telehealth consultations via social media, thus, reaching out to patients in remote areas without access to specialized care. Such advancements will offer avenues for patients not just to receive care, but to have more authority and control over their health management, fostering self-sufficiency and reducing over-reliance on the healthcare system.

9.3. The Ubiquity of Digital Health Marketing

As we examine the future projections, we must heed to the potential ubiquity of digital health marketing spearheaded via social media platforms — becoming the primary facilitator of healthcare communication. With the evolution of AI algorithms, hyper-targeted and personalized health marketing will no longer be a dream, but rather a reality. We envision brands tailoring messages to individuals based on specific health conditions and wellness goals.

Moreover, social media platforms are prophesied to serve as an authentic source of product reviews and testimonials — a dynamic marketplace for health products and services, spinning a new narrative on consumer behavior and brand building in healthcare.

9.4. Regulatory Challenges and Prospects

However, this future comes bundled with challenges, too. We anticipate an increase in concerns surrounding the regulation of this evolving digital space. Policymakers need to evolve right alongside technology, and in some instances, must predict its path ahead of time. The future would call for clearer, directive, and robust regulations to protect patient privacy, confidentiality, and to manage the liability risks involved.

In this complex weave of social media, healthcare, and the impending future, an intricate tapestry of next-generation technology, patient care, health marketing, and regulatory constraints exhibits itself. It's no hesitation that the road ahead for social media in healthcare is potent, exciting, and yet, challenging. Harnessing its potential optimally, responsibly, and ethically calls for a critical yet thoughtful understanding of these underlying dynamics.

In conclusion, while social media is not a remedy for all healthcare challenges, it's indeed a robust tool with colossal potentials. It's crucial not to treat it as a panacea, but instead to perceive it as an empowering device — a catalyst amplifying our capacities to care, communicate, and connect, shaping a resonant healthcare melody that echoes throughout the unforeseen digital healthcare terrain.

Chapter 10. Developing a Winning Social Media Strategy for Healthcare Providers

Establishing a resonant online presence is no less than walking on a tightrope for the healthcare stakeholder. The task becomes even more challenging considering the sensitivities associated with the medical domain. This chapter attempts to thread the needle for healthcare professionals looking to craft a robust social media approach. It breaks down the labyrinth of social media strategy into precise steps and mechanisms that facilitate an influential digital foothold for healthcare providers.

10.1. The Foundation: Understanding the Importance of Social Media in Healthcare

To deeply comprehend the need for a winning social media strategy, it is first essential to understand its importance in the healthcare landscape. One of the primary reasons healthcare providers brace the social media beast is its unprecedented ability to reach out to diverse audiences. From the teenage adolescent grappling with anxieties to the elderly individual battling a chronic condition, social platforms have become the common thread binding them with relevant healthcare information. It also encases a priceless platform for healthcare stakeholders to build their reputation, share their expertise, engage with patients on a personal level, and augment their reach, all contributing to significant improvements in patient satisfaction and health outcomes.

10.2. Step 1: Define Your Goals

Having defined the gravity of social media in healthcare, embarking on the strategy-crafting journey begins with demarcating clear-cut goals. Whether the objective is enhancing patient engagement, improving online reputation, driving website traffic, or increasing awareness about a specific treatment or procedure, each goal should align with the healthcare provider's overall mission and vision.

10.3. Step 2: Identify Your Target Audience

A winning plan is characterized by its resonance with its intended audience. Identifying the target audience's demographics, psychographics, and needs is vital. Understanding the factors such as age, gender, geographic location, health conditions, and digital behaviour of the target audience curtails the possibilities of misdirected communication efforts and paves the way for personalized patient engagement.

10.4. Step 3: Choose the Right Social Media Channels

Shaping a triumphant strategy also commands the appropriate selection of social media channels. While Facebook works excellently for reaching older users, Instagram and Snapchat resonate more with younger demographics. LinkedIn proves fruitful for professional networking and B2B communications. Therefore, the channel selection must be guided by the target audience's digital habits.

10.5. Step 4: Create Engaging Content

The real magic lies in crafting compelling content that ticks with the target group. The content range on social media can fan out from educational blog posts, insightful infographics, emotional patient stories, practical health tips, teasers for upcoming events, to interactive quizzes or polls. It won't be wrong to say, content is the heartbeat of any social media strategy.

10.6. Step 5: Engage with Your Audience

Social media extends beyond one-way communication. Audience engagement becomes the propelling force catapulting the healthcare provider's reputation. Prompt and polite responses to comments, queries, reviews, or shares helps cultivate a personalized patient-provider relationship building trust.

10.7. Step 6: Monitor, Analyze, and Optimize

Last but not least, inserting analytics into strategic planning is a necessary element. Regular monitoring and evaluation of social media metrics guide any necessary amendments or improvements. Tools like Google Analytics, Hootsuite, or Sprout Social streamline the analysis of social media campaigns.

10.8. Some Word of Caution: Social Media Ethics and Regulations

While social media unfurls limitless opportunities, it also opens a Pandora's box of ethical and legal issues. Confidentiality breaches, misinformation, unprofessional behaviour, or non-compliance with guidelines can toss reputational and legal challenges. Awareness and adherence to Health Insurance Portability and Accountability Act (HIPAA) regulations and platform-specific policies cushion against such pitfalls.

In conclusion, wrapping a winning social media strategy for healthcare providers demands a balance between understanding the audience, crafting compelling content, engaging with the community, and constantly optimizing while abiding by ethical standards and regulations. The journey may be riddled with challenges, but the destination sure leads to an empowered and enlightened health sphere.

Chapter 11. Lessons and Recommendations: Optimizing Social Media in Healthcare Management

Ever since its inception, social media has candidly reshaped our interactions contributing heavily not only to how we communicate individually, socially, and professionally, but also how we negotiate with healthcare management. As this digital platform interweaves itself compellingly into these paradigms, it is becoming increasingly important to understand how its optimal utilization can best catalyze the intricate mechanics of healthcare management. Hence, a comprehensive distillation of the key elements, effective strategies, and best practices enabling the effective integration of social media into this sector become essential in empowering healthcare providers and industry professionals. This chapter aims to shed light on these thought-provoking insights, unfolding a pragmatic tapestry that illustrates the streams converging social media and healthcare management.

11.1. Strategically Mapping and Integrating Social Media in Healthcare Management

Fundamentally, the successful deployment of social media strategies within healthcare management necessitates rigorous planning and strategic mapping. A one-size-fits-all blueprint is never the answer. Thus, healthcare providers should design a roadmap based on their unique objectives, patient demographics, and resources. It's worthwhile to consider the type of content you want to share, the platforms that resonate best with your target population, the tone of voice to use, and other crucial factors. Genuine patient stories, healthcare tips, regular updates, and interactive multimedia content can significantly bolster online presence and patient engagement, promoting a holistic, patient-centered approach in healthcare management. Furthermore, knowing the best times to post content can have an impact on visibility and engagement.

11.2. Building a Sustainable, Authentic Online Presence

Having a profound, sustainable digital footprint can significantly enhance the brand image and reputation of a healthcare provider. However, such a feat should not lean on the sheer frequency of social media posts. Instead, it necessitates fostering an authentic relationship with your audience, facilitated by timely, relevant, and empathetic engagement with patient queries and feedback, and sharing credible, verified health information created or endorsed by medical professionals. Authentic interaction serves as the bedrock for trust-building, essential for any healthcare institution. Additionally, all healthcare communication must adhere to HIPAA compliance, vehemently safeguarding patient information privacy.

11.3. Navigating the Privacy and Ethical Conundrums

One of the most formidable challenges is the ethical rigmarole and privacy concerns associated with disseminating health care information via social platforms. Confidentiality and privacy of patient information are paramount, making it compulsory for healthcare organizations to maintain strong privacy policies in line with relevant laws and regulations, including HIPAA in the U.S. and GDPR in Europe. Furthermore, providers are expected to act ethically and professionally, just as they would in any face-to-face interaction, further ensuring trust and integrity.

11.4. Promoting Engagement Through Innovative Technologies

The employment of cutting-edge technology can help nurture better patient engagement and foster a more interactive online presence. Live video sessions, augmented reality features, utilization of chatbots for patient inquiries, and webinars with health specialists are just a few of the innovative methods to facilitate a more dynamic, open channel that can revolutionize the healthcare management realm.

11.5. Efficacious Use of Data Analytics

Accurate, data-driven insights are pivotal to optimizing a social media strategy and fine-tuning the way providers engage online. Data analytics can identify patterns in patient behavior, preferences, and needs, helping shape content and strategies tuned for maximal engagement. However, while scavenging through the troves of data, adherence to data protection norms is obligatory to preserve the sensitive nature of healthcare-related information.

In conclusion, successfully optimizing social media in healthcare management is a vast and complex endeavour, one that requires a nuanced understanding of the delicate interplay between digital communication, medical professionalism, patient engagement, and privacy norms. By strategically harnessing the empyreal reaches of social media, healthcare providers can realize a truly transformational shift in their management paradigms, fostering a more patient-centric, responsive, and communicative sphere which is the lofty aspiration of modern-day healthcare.